FIVE WAYS TO KILL A MAN

EDWIN BROCK

FIVE WAYS TO KILL A MAN

New and Selected Poems

ENITHARMON PRESS 1990

First published in 1990
by the Enitharmon Press
40 Rushes Road
Petersfield
Hampshire GU32 3BW

© Edwin Brock 1990

ISBN 1 870612 16 7 (paper)
ISBN 1 870612 21 3 (cloth)

Set in 10pt Bembo by Bryan Williamson, Darwen
and printed by
Antony Rowe Limited, Chippenham, Wiltshire

Illustrations by Elizabeth Brock

CONTENTS

From *Here. Now. Always.* (1977)

WHEN MY FATHER DIED

On the day my father died
 all the hoops in the neighbourhood rang
 skate wheels shrilled on summer pavements
 and I in my blakey-boots clanged one foot
  in each gutter

On the day my father died
 girls were running autumn-eyed, with wild hair
 and hands of silk; peg-tops had come round again
 and in the sky the angels were as plain as wings

But on the day my father died
 white faces fell from every window
 and every house found rooms of tears to hide
 while I, joy-jumping, empty-eyed sang on the day
  my father died

Now my father dies a little every day
And the faces from each window grow like mine.

AN ATTEMPT AT EXORCISM

Now it is your yellow dress and young
sun-coloured legs that I remember
and the Old Bridge in Dulwich Park
and the ducks being noisy about summer

and this, though false, is something which persists
like the jammed note of a car-horn in
a long and lonely street, and the one and only
memory of drowning, which also is untrue.

For now I can no longer shuffle you
from memory, but turn up Jokers in my hand
along with Kings and Queens. Of course
there may have been no yellow dress

and the Old Bridge, which is now made
of stone, is also suspect. Perhaps
only ducks, then, and their noisy summers
still exist; that and your yellow-coloured legs.

IN MEMORY OF MY FATHER

This is said to please someone I never
consciously pleased, someone whom
I carry with me here or there, or take
out from my pocket and examine carefully.

But when the sun shines, accurate and
clear, there is nothing I remember;
nothing which I could not draw as well
from a memory of other people, or swear

that this was so because it is ennobling
or pure; yet purity and nobleness are
nothing here, so that really I begin
within a sort of emptiness, and hope

that slowly I may probe it out. Despite
this you appear always to be telling me
some inappropriately tiny thing: a way
to handle knives and forks or comb my hair.

I presume we cannot always have been eating,
or preening half-forgotten heads in bedrooms.
In fact I do recall that once we walked
together past a well-known grammar school

and you insisted on and on that I make this
a kind of goal. Although you never knew,
it was a goal I scored – though nobody bothered
about it very much, least of all me.

And that I suppose is our main difficulty:
that the image that I make you have of me
is one that you would never have enjoyed;
and yet continually I wish that you were here,

if only that we talked on knives and forks:
it is a sort of emptiness I bear; it is
a kind of charm which never works and which,
in dragging from my pocket, I may tear.

A CLUTTER OF MOTHERS

Many-clothed and smelling of cheap soap
are all the mothers I have known;
many-mouthed, loudly critical and alone.

Not often pregnant, they appear always
in a horde of children begging at
sweet-counters; not often rich, they swear

that every mouthful is the last. I have loved
all mothers from time to time: mother
Church, mother Hubbard and poor old

mother Brock, yet I will never understand
why every woman taking my dumb hand
between her own remains so true to type:

many-mouthed, loudly critical, alone,
declaring that the best is always past
and swearing that each mouthful is my last.

UNLUCKY JIM

My father was a man who laughed at charms
Walked under ladders and whistled at the wind
Who would not turn his silver at the moon's command
Nor cross his breast when freed from mortal sin.

My father was a man among all men
Threw bullseye darts in grinning public bars
Who seven-nightly at the call of ten
Would hang his paper hat upon the stars.

And daily I have seen my mother sit
With knives uncrossed beside a silver gnome
Polishing St Christopher with salt and spit
To hold the wind that hauls the traveller home.

But all the luck in all the lonely world
And all the double-darts and wringing hands
Were far away the day my father died
Or saw him fall and would not understand.

AFTER CHRISTMAS

It was later than Christmas
    a January snow as round as sparrows' eggs
    fell like feathers, and I was knee-high glad that it was so.

It was later than Christmas
    and no one in the half-dark world as long as
    a year and a year to go was there to share a thing.

It was only my mother
    my father and myself stepped high and slowly where
    the winter year began to flow in feathered January.

It was only my first
    and now my only memory; the year began and ended then
    in January, in darkness, and in snow.

It was later than Christmas
    and when Christmas had come round again the snow had gone
    and there were merely years repeating what was known.

'...and the mother let them look as much as they chose,
for green is good for the eyes.' The Ugly Duckling

Mother ducks are wiser than they know:
    Before the duckling walks or swims or flies
She leans her head towards the earth to show
    The green that will grow golden in his eyes.

Our all-too-human mothers disagree
    And ache to give us pink and blue and red,
Conduct us on a colour-climbing spree
    Which will luxuriate our imitating head,

And then it takes a boyhood and a bit
    To cool our minds and see things as they are:
To make the eyeballs patient to admit
    The green that grows us hair by reaching hair.

In worldliness the mother duck succeeds
    Where we have stumbled – feeling out so far
To stake a claim on tinselled time, which leads
    A life away to find things as they are.

A QUIET NIGHT

It was a quiet night, you will remember:
warm, with a little mist among the trees;
we had left two children sleeping; the ease
of ten years' loving was between. You were
in a broken mood, remember? I talked
as though I understood the world; the mist
between the trees, concealing lovers, kissed
your mood and pulled your hair uncurled. We walked

where we had been before we married; quiet
it was with my voice droning on; ten years
I talked away before I carried your mood
and you to where the grass was long, and tight
our love became to loose your worries,
as soft your song becomes when I intrude.

FIVE WAYS TO KILL A MAN

There are many cumbersome ways to kill a man:
you can make him carry a plank of wood
to the top of a hill and nail him to it. To do this
properly you require a crowd of people
wearing sandals, a cock that crows, a cloak
to dissect, a sponge, some vinegar and one
man to hammer the nails home.

Or you can take a length of steel,
shaped and chased in a traditional way,
and attempt to pierce the metal cage he wears.
But for this you need white horses,
English trees, men with bows and arrows,
at least two flags, a prince and
a castle to hold your banquet in.

Dispensing with nobility, you may, if the wind
allows, blow gas at him. But then you need
a mile of mud sliced through with ditches,
not to mention black boots, bomb craters,
more mud, a plague of rats, a dozen songs
and some round hats made of steel.

In an age of aeroplanes, you may fly
miles above your victim and dispose of him by
pressing one small switch. All you then
require is an ocean to separate you, two
systems of government, a nation's scientists,
several factories, a psychopath and
land that no one needs for several years.

These are, as I began, cumbersome ways
to kill a man. Simpler, direct, and much more neat
is to see that he is living somewhere in the middle
of the twentieth century, and leave him there.

CATASTROPHE

I destroyed the first cat we had:
crammed her into a basket one spring-wet
day and walked angrily to the vet. 'Do away
with her,' I said. 'For a year we've tried
to train her, and the flat is full of fishbones
and catshit.' The second cat, a small grey
one that I loved, pined for the first one
and died a month later. After that
there was a succession of cats, dying
from cat-flu, dysentry, pregnancy
and motor cars. I suppose we were fond of them.

If the first cat had lived, the second one
would not have died; nor would the others
have followed. There are times
when I feel a kind of Eichmann of cats,
and pray that it will not be the same
with wives. Whether she destroyed me
or I her is irrelevant. She must not be
the first to die of treachery, adultery,
pregnancy or suicide. One could easily
acquire a taste for this kind of living.
I watch the way I treat my children – carefully.

THE BIRD WITH MOTHER

'Don't do it,' they all said in the same dull
adult voice – just as they had always done about
everything. And it was this that made me draw my
seventeen years before me to witness my discretion.
'How can you be a sailor,' I said 'without at least
one tattoo?' And they shook their heads,
their mouse-brown adult heads, in unison.

I'll say this for them, the shop itself did
nearly put me off. Tucked in a Chatham sidestreet,
it was no bigger than my mother's kitchen.
There were bare boards upon the floor, tattoos
in frames upon the walls, and an old man
with dirty fingers scratching marks upon
a soldier's arm. My mate and I watched his blood
glisten along the lines the needle made.
'I'm not having *that* done,' he said, and I
was afraid to go back upon myself.
Pretty soon it was too late anyway – with my
shirt-sleeve rolled and my white arm held
tightly in the old man's fingers. 'What
d'you want?' he said, not seeming to have much
time to spare, and I said 'A bird with mother,'
that being the first thing that came to mind.

Now, in kindness to my family, I wear
my shirt-sleeves down upon the hottest summer
day, and scrub that part of me with peroxide.
Nothing fades it, and in a way I like it
to be there. It comforts me to know, in moments
of despair, that I am only, ever,
the total sum of everything I've done.

A MOMENT OF RESPECT

Two things I remember about my grandfather:
his threadbare trousers, and the way he adjusted
his half-hunter watch two minutes every day.

When I asked him why he needed to know the time so
exactly, he said a business man could lose a fortune
by being two minutes late for an appointment.

When he died he left two meerschaum pipes
and a golden sovereign on a chain. Somebody
threw the meerschaum pipes away, and
there was an argument about the sovereign.

On the day of his burial the church clock chimed
as he was lowered down into the clay, and all
the family advanced their watches by two minutes.

CURTAINS, DOORS AND A BED

Curtains left too long at a window
rot. Something in the air it seems
causes holes with too much looking.

A bed that is slept in too long
stinks. Something in the atmosphere
objects to this confinement.

A room with a closed door collects
dust. The pages of the books there
curl through lack of use.

Nobody has suitably explained
why the curtains and the doors in my house
suffer these indignities.

Nor why, when I throw them open and
unmake my bed, the rain walks in
to settle down beside me.

AN IDYLL

Now, on this first Sunday of sunshine
we make this pilgrimage to be where
grass and bushes show the season in.

There is blossom there: the white sort
and the red; dogs; and by the lake one duck
treads upon another for our pleasure.

There is movement: of birds behind leaves;
worms beneath earth; and families
which were unrecognisable before Lowry.

We are not aware of how we fit into
the scene; after an hour we feel boredom, take
a last look at the trodden duck, and go away.

Pigeons come daily to the yard behind
my mother's flat. No sun shines
on them; no rainbowed necklet
decorates that puff of down. Occasionally
a squall of rain disturbs them but,
apart from that, they move like fat
grey triangles upon the ground.

On three sides they are surrounded by
tall-storied houses uniformly grey;
on the fourth a kind of lean-to shed
for backstreet engineering. Upon the
paving stones the fair-haired children
still fall about and play; and, farther off
the main road traffic sounds.
It makes no difference to these birds
what day of week it is – it only seems
that there are more on Sundays.
And though the creatures must
make love, this is managed
somewhere else. Here, it is just
some quality of dust that entertains them.
From the same cracked window I have
watched them now for twenty years –
and prayed that, one spring day,
a neighbouring cat would find them.

ONLY CHILD

At the age of eight I practised levitation:
laid in bed and willed myself six inches
from the ceiling. Underneath me
the ground was dead; some pale-faced

boy slept in my bed; I would have known
if he had been my brother. Regularly
at night my parents came to this one,
kissed him carefully and curled the clothes

about him. I was not aware of love
or anything like that: we did not fight,
this boy and I, nor did I begrudge him
their attention. Call it what you like,

that nightly jaunt I took, analyse it
as you will, there must have been
some benefit I gained from it – otherwise
I'd have come down long ago.

SUNDAY P.M.

Then, there were peacocks on
the bowling green; other families
than my own stared at eyes
until the dark came out

and threadbare dogs would wander to
the confab at the concrete pool
which, yearly drained, would show
dead cracks and darker weed.

This seed of Sundays holds on me
and sets me restlessly about
the trees that hang in dust-sheets;
still I stare until the dark comes out.

Ours is a need for showy endings:
upon my children's faces is a shout
that kills all peacocks,
sets the dogs to rout.

PRETTY AS A PICTURE

For a portrait I would have a head
such as my son draws, with round eyes,
a line nose, and ears that hear nothing –
for my son is a realist and I do not inhabit

his obsessional world. For a portrait
I would have this picture, being proud
only of its truth – for I am not shrewd
and I do not conduct myself at all.

There are times between meeting and
meeting when I am obsessional, when
the ordinary holds only a gasp of
apprehension, and I wonder if this is true.

I cannot call it heaven or hell; it is
obsessional and, if I could draw it,
it would be round, with a line nose which does not
smell, and would be called a portrait of me.

INDIA

Gandhi sat in India
cross-legged by a spinning wheel;
'Gandhi will get you if you
don't behave,' my mother said.

Gandhi sat in a cinema
cross-legged on a newsreel;
if I didn't behave he'd come
for me, dressed up in a ghost-sheet.

I wasn't afraid of Gandhi
(worse things happen at the cinema)
but I kept quiet about it,
not wanting to worry my mother.

There are snakes in India
played by men with bandaged heads;
the snakes could have frightened me,
except I'd got used to the cinema by then.

I didn't think too much about India
for a good many years, because in London
you can get along without India
most of your life.

When I got around to India again
a lot of things had changed: I was
sitting in my bedroom, cross-legged,
trying to feel like Gandhi in a ghost-sheet.

But you live without India
far too long, all dressed up in a city suit,
and sitting cross-legged on your bedroom
floor doesn't feel like Gandhi at all.

The last time I thought about India
the *Kama Sutra* was out in paperback,
but trying to read it with a slipped disc
and a paunchy waist was difficult.

So I decided there and then
to give up India. I'm thinking about it
now: it's a kind of frieze
with Gandhi playing a bull-necked snake

cross-legged by a spinning wheel
while millions of temple women lie down
before him to make a footpath
all the way up to Nirvana.

India's a nice kind of fantasy,
but Gandhi's dead, and you can be sold
the *Kama Sutra* in a Butlin's camp
by one of those nice red-coated girls.

On a quiet Sunday
when the sun is out
you can drive to
a village in Kent
which boasts a
coffee bar with plastic
tables. Among the
paraphernalia on the
walls a bird in a
painted cage says
Ban the bomb ban
the bomb ban the
bomb ban the bomb.
Boys in shiny jackets
fidget there with
beehive girls. The chickens
look brittle and taste
as though they were made
in the same factory
as the tabletops.

We can't grumble about accommodation:
we have a new concrete floor that's
always dry, four walls that are
painted white, and a sheet-iron roof
the rain drums on. A fan blows warm air
beneath our feet to disperse the smell
of chickenshit and, on dull days,
fluorescent lighting sees us.

You can tell me: if you come by
the north door, I am in the twelfth pen
on the left-hand side of the third row
from the floor; and in that pen
I am usually the middle one of three.
But, even without directions, you'd
discover me. I have the same orange-
red comb, yellow beak and auburn
feathers, but as the door opens and you
hear above the electric fan a kind of
one-word wail, I am the one
who sounds loudest in my head.

Listen. Outside this house there's an
orchard with small moss-green apple
trees; beyond that, two fields of
cabbages; then, on the far side of
the road, a broiler house. Listen:
one cockerel grows out of there, as
tall and proud as the first hour of sun.
Sometimes I stop calling with the others
to listen, and wonder if he hears me.

The next time you come here, look for me.
Notice the way I sound inside my head.
God made us all quite differently,
and blessed us with this expensive home.

ADMAN RELAXING

Talking to four men
    who are
listening to three men
    who are
talking to two men
    who are
listening to one man
    who is
saying that
it is easier
to hump
a camel
through
the kingdom
of heaven
than talk
to four men
who are
listening

A MAN OF THE WORLD

Zen is a man
in a backstreet
making small bells
for girls
in the Kings Road.

Beauty is Twiggy
in a fun-fur
drawing crossed ells
in a bankbook.

Love is a Mars bar
stuffed between expensive thighs.
Ambition is Wilson
and there is Frost for God.

I am thankful
that I can contain Zen
in this small concept
being able to define
and dismiss it
in the same few words.

And I am proud
that there is nothing
you can think of
I cannot similarly reduce
to the same small essence.

These are my credentials:
I am clever
and I am aware.

You buy me
in a small transparent ball
almost entirely filled with water.
You shake me
and a plastic snowstorm
will ensue.

Having learned
to draw
dark glasses
and a fair
simulation
of hair
you need only
one brushful
of that white paint
which does not
drip
covers in one coat
and dries
in a day
to a hard gloss
surface
which is washable
and will last
a lifetime.

EPITAPH

The Octopus is a loathsome creature,
encompassing another in its sucker-grip
for satisfaction. If, however, you
bite it between the eyes, it will die.
I have two teeth marks
equidistant from the bridge of my nose.

ROSE GARDEN

The god-machine is on roses today
and I am trying to do my job properly:
'Red, Yellow, Pink,' I say
'Blackspot, Rust and Mildew':
it is a tedious task making catalogues
and I do not know whether Orthocide
and Dithane are part of the plan.

I try very hard to appreciate:
'Red, Yellow, Pink,' I say
with a catch in my voice and my face
arranged like Mary's at the Annunciation.
I am no fool: I have learned
when the bells ring and my hands are burned
from touching too many bare wires.

God has this good plan about roses
which requires only open eyes and a smile:
'Red, Yellow, Pink,' I say, smiling,
for the burns are still there
and I would like to use my hands again.
Do you see how each rose offers you
its own colour, requiring only
that its roots shall feel some death
to feed upon, and that you should
die for it and enjoy the process.

God has this good plan about roses
and about people, that they should look
and smile and die and enjoy it. I am no fool:
'People,' I say 'Red, Yellow, Pink,'
and Mary and I have smiled until
every muscle in our faces aches and
we have tried enjoying it. But
our hands are heavily bandaged now

and sometimes at night I dream
that I have made it up. It is,
after all, something to do under the sun,
this looking at roses, it is something
to doubt; and with our hands bandaged
we can hold the wire and stare out
to where the world began.

FOX AT WINTERTON

All night the gale
had brought glass
wood and bodies
from the sea
using sand to make
a decent burial

leaving the beach
as ordered as
an Esher cemetery
each mound a mystery
except where a wing
or beak broke through
like weed.

I gave each one
a casual rite
dispensing death
like a clergyman
until I stopped
at a shape
as shocking as
a scream in church:

its red fur
stained the sand,
its head was chewed
into a fanged skull
and ten inches of rope
grew from its spine

yet enough of fox
remained to make
me flinch
expecting the massacre

to jump up and snap and
infect my clean skin
with God knows what wounds.

Even walking away
I looked back
unless its stumps
stalked me along the beach:

not until another month
of tides had turned
its tame bones
would I accept it.

This creature contained
so much life
its death shrieked,
shaming the quiet cough
that takes us
so barely alive
the air settles
where we were
without a sound.

THE GREAT POSE

No more pictures,
unless the ghosts appear:
I am trying
to do without ghosts.

How many times
I've said one field
one tree and a broken hare
or stood on a beach
and taken one wave –

it's impossible...
I make the buggers up!
I've got a tree-
making hare-breaking
sea-machine in my head
turning out prototypes...
the *things* are never there!

And yet at this time of year
when the roads are empty
I come to this coast
like a hippy to a banyan tree
and stand on the cliff-edge
facing the sea
saying Do it, do it!

On the shingle below me
three men fish
a small ship takes forever
to cross the horizon
the wind blows gulls about
and two dogs chase
along the tide foam.
Do it, I say
and fix those men, that ship
and the dogs in memory.

For a time
I talk more life into them
than ever the wind or the sea made
until the weather changes and they fade
back into the machinery.

Oh I have fixed you and you there
staring as you talk
even closing my eyes
to see you better
and when I bring you back
you have more flesh
than I've felt before:

I have more dead cats living with me
than I ever owned
I have made more fathers
than made me
and all my gods have fine feathers
and strong arms.

I stand in the middle of this making
as frightened as a child
before pain
or rather it was the pain
took me there
and I am making the child,
or perhaps the pain
is being nothing there
and contrarily I make it to hurt.

All these things are possible and happen.

It is tempting to call this a journey,
to stick both thumbs
in my grandfather's pocket and look back;

but always the sun yo-yos up and down
and nothing happens.

You, yourself, are nowhere.

Three men fish from a shingle beach
the wind blows gulls about them
and two small dogs chase a ship
across the horizon.

Someone has made something up.

And this, surprisingly
is the world's machine:
grass, flowers, birds and fish
are churned from our feet
without dread. Look, I am walking
in a small field; there is rain
on leaves and spiders' webs; mice, birds
cows, lions and men steam in the sunshine.
Nothing approaches me. The field
is there forever and in a year
I may return to feel it.

Every weed has its own beauty
and not least because each year
it greens its straws;
white and yellow flowers appear
not to be seen but to seed; runners
reach out and rear up, couch grass
grows in my hair and my toes take root.

Now the field returns to me: mice
birds, lions and men steam in the sunshine.
I approach nothing and I am not approached.
But my fear falls and fertilises
and my loneliness loves.

L.E.B.

In 1965 you bounced
like a blonde Tigger
into a life whose
spring had snapped:

you began in a night-
club bouncing men
with bald heads;

you bounced a totem-
pole from the Old
Year to the New;

you bounced into
pregnancy into hospital
and bounced back

bouncing a baby whose
beginning could so easily
have been flat;

you bounced through
the Divorce Court bounced
a Judge off his bench

and bounced into home-
making as though the walls
were made of rubber;

you made sinning
seem merely a lack
of bounce

and when your time comes
you will leave us all
like a ball
we lost in childhood.

T.A.L.

There were always bombers overhead
when topless in old trousers
you played The Lost Chord
on a piano accordion
with your biceps

it was the same tune you played
when you punched the carthorse silly
and broke a navvy's nose
with the heel of your boot

what tunes you must have heard
and tried to squeeze through
that Swiss bauble!
Wagner at least
blew you through Burma
and back to break holes
in the bedroom door

and all the time you were playing
The Lost Chord and What'll I Do
When You Are Far Away

until with the accordion pawned
you packed your bags and
rode to where we heard
the same tunes fading

and wondered whether it was
not knowing what to hum
made you break teeth
black eyes and leave weals
upon your daughter's bum
which now mark her womanhood.

H.D. & F.D.

He swallowed raw eggs
floating in spiced vinegar

she crunched peanut brittle;

he had a stern portrait
of himself in the First War

she had fat holiday snaps;

he taught his sons to fight
upright like gentlemen

she bounced their children;

his bearing was like
an old Prussian gone to seed

hers like an Irish potato;

he cooked, gardened and shouted
at her whenever she tried

she grumbled inarticulately;

the family watched this performance
quietly taking sides

and afterwards laughed at the joke;

but once when she cried
I saw through the laughter

and when she died

he coughed for ten more years
without raising a smile.

FROM CHIPPING NORTON

In these lanes
are edges
which are always damp

under an old stone
at the end of a wall
a mile between houses
where either grey creatures
start life or life fades
in cold grey creatures.

These hills in England
with green coverings
and stone journeys
grow numbness
at the ends of their extremities

as though that were the beginning
of a certain route
where we go
like a monk praying.

They are damp litanies
the voice croaks on
but sings:

the road rises and falls
turns and returns
but takes time.

It is a cold way
except where skin
closer than houses
forms wife, mother, daughter
and warms you there.

PROTOTYPES

1

King George the Fifth
looked like my grandfather
and felt as close

when he died
I walked the streets
staring at houses

and their faces
to see if people
looked the same and

their homes still stood.
For a week
we were on the brink

of war or an earthquake
and when my mother
laughed at me

I abandoned her
to God's anger
or soldiers from the Tower.

King George the Fifth
was my first and last king,
his children

and their children
were never properly introduced
and I ignored them.

2

My father played the piano
with one finger of his right hand
and the fist of his left

he laughed at Gracie Fields
Max Miller and was away from home
for weeks at a time

when he died I cried
for my mother
and forgot.

I have never mastered the art
of becoming my father:
I have three children

pale jackets, suede shoes
and laugh at comedians
I do not admire

I stay away from home
for weeks at a time
but I do not resemble him.

When he came home
he brought himself with him
and sat down

when I arrive
I hit the piano with both hands
and nothing happens.

3
Britannia glowed
from Empire Day
all the way to Barry Road

a big-girl jumped over
her skipping rope
and walked away on her hands

on Saturday night
I jumped over a saxophone
and ran among mad skirts

by Sunday I had married the girl
next door and all the saxophones
played the Last Post.

4
On my bedside table
is a triptych
of a king, a father and a wife

at night I sleep
with one eye open
hoping to surprise them

I am wrong:
their dead faces
fill all my gaps

and nothing happens
except I contain them,
father-king and dancing-wife

they have killed my ear
for saxophones
and nobody, not even

Fred Astaire, could take
his toes to a brass band
playing a requiem mass.

SUMMER VISIT

All our maps have these small crosses
with an arrow at the top
to show where God went:
something about birds falling
trees bending, rain, hail and snow.
Down here I keep it behind glass
to switch on and off like a toy.

Forty years darkness is thick here:
rain has fallen and in damp places
fingers grow. My mother blinks
in sunlight, her roots making cracks
I can never explore.

I am afraid. This place is not
situated but grows around
wherever I am. Sometimes
I make it move and move into it
pretending to be real.
My mother watches and waits to begin.

Nothing changes: voice and weather
drift in the same direction.
A mad dog climbs the kitchen wall
and dies. A coffin is balanced
between two chairs. The sky
is low and flat and my mother's noise
fills the space beneath it.

Time shrinks and stretches
without rhyme or reason. I am the child
I saw in a seaside snap: I make
donkeys move, hear my mother
call and let memory happen.
Nothing happens, except the tapeworm
fear between us eats and grows fat.

HISTORY

Over and
over some
thing like
wind is
whipping
through our
two conifers

as though
the walls
had allowed
crows in
or perhaps
the sky
had decided
against us.

And I really
did know
a man who
ran amok
with knives
and was
certified

(he was
a quiet man
who played
with my
daughter
and mended
bicycles).

Now that
he has gone
the wind
is no less
and over
and over
the crows
accuse us
with knives.

Nothing is
ever defined.
Mostly
I make
my life
leave on time
and carry me
home again.

The crows
fly quietly
in my pocket

the sky
is undecided

and my daughter
no longer
plays with
men who
mend bicycles.

DEATH IN NOVEMBER

(In memory of Matthew Brock)

Month of the dead fly,
and maggots dormant in stiff grass

month of the burned guy,
abandoned nests and iron frost

month when the old year
twists upon young throats

cold of the hanged year and
Christmas lights switched on by ghosts

when death, too much for tiny shoulders,
suffocates a son who leaves
singing in the early morning
and prayer before sleep

who made even suffering seem boy-size
by telling in a two-year voice
dwarfing grief we make enormous
to fill a lifetime's loss

whose memory makes us regret
the intellect that breaks belief:
today we threw a Christmas toy away
and bought a wreath.

THE BONSAI POEM

If you take an acorn
and plant it in
a small container
with a drainage hole,
you may train the seedling
into a gnarled oak
only ten inches high

this is done by
leaf-stripping
shoot-pinching
and lifting the tree
from its bed each winter
to trim the roots

by the careful choice
of container and
a thoughtful use
of stone and moss
you strive for a strained look,
a tortured look
the look of a tree
which has fought its environment
for a nightmare survival

you may attain
in ten years or so
the ravages of a century:
summers of lightning
winters of hard frost
and the burning
of a salt-sharp wind

yet all the time
your oak has been screened
in a formal garden
syringed in summer and
pruned with fine polished knives

half closing your eyes
you may one day dream yourself
into its shade
having found it suffering
in some god-forsaken
corner of England

and if when your dream ends
you find yourself
in proportion to the old-young tree
in some god-forsaken corner
gnarled, trimmed and ten times
your age, your years of patience
will have brought you
face to face
with the psychology of loss.

A FORMULA FOR SUCCESS

If you put one leg
ahead of your body
balance on it and swing
the other you move
a yard forward

this takes one second
of your life.

If you put one sunrise
ahead of your vision
balance on it and swing
forward you move
into nightfall

this takes one day
of your life.

Similarly weeks
months and years
may be annihilated
with practice

until a lifetime
passes without pain.

The trick is in balance
and momentum
always keeping your eyes
on horizons and your mind
on a goal

until moving demonstrates
horizons and goals.

Mostly you will travel
through people
without contact
for contact is not
essential to progress

but in event of contact
it must be swift
heavy and irreversible
so that momentum
is not checked

this technique
once acquired
will carry you through
all institutions
whether domestic
or social.

Failures will occur
through striking others
when off balance
or catching an eye
at point of contact

this causes relationship
and breaks momentum.

Try always
to sleep deeply
and without dreaming
remembering
when dreams occur
that they have
no meaning

dress well
eat well and be
always moving
for there are horizons
everywhere
continually travelling
at your own good speed.

(Inspired artist. Mongol. Died in an institution
because the experts measured his brain)

His fingers
were like deaf ears
and he smelt
of institutions

his eyes
were an old torch
pitted with
corrosion

Red, he said
Green, stabbing
the chalk with
deaf fingers

to make a line
as alive
as Beethoven's
last Quartet.

We believed
he worked so close
because his blind eyes
failed him

but he knew
without knowing
that his heart
could only fall that far.

DIAGNOSIS

I have a Swiss watch
my neighbour's is Japanese
side by side at night
we turn them
like skilled undertakers

our calendar shows
the day a strange man died
but does not show
how many
have gone since then

at six o'clock
a photograph
talks about disasters:
we watch and worry
and take our clocks away

we do not understand
why we grow roses
touch each other
and sometimes try
to simulate a storm

we have strong doctors
fast aeroplanes
and live in layers
like communal graves

there is much death
about us but it is not
our own, therefore
it is not death
and we can describe it

'you will die but I
will not die' is what
we say side by side:
this is our strength
and our civilization

our plague
is the blocked heart
but we are not afraid:
one day we will make
a nursery song
for the photograph
to sing, and then
we will all fall down.

NOVEMBER

Long summer loosens now
the speedboats and the girls depart
shaved stubble shows its skull
and the first mists start
a comfortable loneliness.

Dead oaks align themselves
like markers on the marshes
and flat farms, and docile ducks
with winter coughs
sound storybook alarms.

Wait. It will happen.
Watch the way the sky expands
not reaching out but running from
small hands freezing as
they squeeze prayer.

Behind barns and breakwaters
some corner of the weather
slips to where
the North Sea sways
weed and shingle.

Offshore a seal pup barks
and beaches itself upon rough sand
his slashed belly baring
like a broken hand
this year's sacrifice.

PASTORAL

It is no commonplace thing
this East Coast beach where I have heard
Beethoven's cellos reverberating
and my mother shrieking like a seabird

years ago I would sing
skipping a perpendicular suicide
knowing as I crashed God would decide
one-handed to set me back laughing

now He's gone, not dead but slow in middle age
there's no alternative but do the thing yourself
already flying has improved my mother's health
and ghosts are thickening at the sea's edge

I'll set the whole environment in concrete
God left the job half-done in empty air
how else should I excuse a life's defeat
this beach becomes the rush-hour in Trafalgar Square.

INHERITANCE

The mummies
were our Saturday treat
and we saved them till last

took in first
the Iron Maiden
the stuffed owls
and the suit of armour
on a plaster horse

then at the end of a corridor
of lighted fishtanks
stood and frightened ourselves
with the long bandaged limb
and its tarry head.

If you spent the night here
you'd be mad by morning:
this we knew as surely
as summer holidays and winter fogs.

Two things bothered me:
why they were called mummies
and what wounded flesh I'd find
if I stripped the cloth away.

Unbandaging myself today
I knew the answers:

as I peeled my mother
from my hands and feet
the white flesh looked
the same but had no feeling

and scraping the usual smile
from its round mirror
I counted those who had
spent the night there
and been mad by morning.

AFTER INNOCENCE

Why did we ever move away
from anywhere?

There were always those moments
of small holes in the air
I thought were atoms.

Nothing was ever solid – not
on those old corners where
we passed through each other
like ghosts in a light wind.

Names and places didn't matter:
things were so open we exchanged
each other at any time,
and time was mostly one more day
without an ending.

But slowly we have moved away
and this is the strangeness of it all:
there may be others who have moved
into the holes we left

who find, in trying to pass through
each other, they smash buildings
uproot trees and destroy the air.

THE RIVER AND THE TRAIN

On this journey I choose
a sidecarriage, preferring
a cell's solitary to those
adolescents in the long hut.

By my left eye the landscape
is at slack tide: trees and barns
barely flowing in a thick swell;
soon it will turn, carrying us
south on a regular current.

A thumbnail of moon hangs
just that space from Venus
Miro drew, and I pump
a barrier of blood to keep
my eyes awake.

Love stays on these words
describing a line like
circumference. Oh I tug
and if it breaks, something
not myself goes free.

Breath holds for what seems
a longer moment, and
this is immortality;
so many people I knew jumped
before the river ran again.

This circling water made our
first measuring, and now we hope
that if we call the god benign
he will not insist on sacrifice.

But I recall a woman who cried
that she must die to give
her daughter living space
and it is her tears I drown in.

HOLY COW

There is a Grandma Moses cow
across the road: black and white
with a kind of gingham antimacassar
draped on her back.

I want this cow in a green surround
framed upon my wall: not exactly
as I see her now but in a way
I cannot see her because of my
bad relationship with God

which is something I can't explain
but which the cow, being an icon,
may modify for perhaps an hour.

There are other cows in the field,
deep dykes, sharp thistles and
a wind which makes the grass shiver.

Sometimes I say, 'Cow, grass, wind,'
over and over as though when I stop
something will go on. It is silly.

The angel floats across offering
her nose for breath but because
of my bad relationship with God
the field stops and the cows ridicule
the belief that anything was there.

THE COWS LET OUT

Like fat women in a field
like fat women in topless dresses
like playful women prancing
through new grass and clover

in middle-age she skipped
salt-mustard-vinegar-pepper
her M&S bra straining
to contain its flying flesh

then breathless with exertion
smiled her shyness up at
the neighbour's bland windows

in this first sunstruck silliness
both cows and skipping woman
jumped sexuality out of
its most unlikely bed

and remembering it now I
cling to the reassurance
that our shapes cannot
imprison us, and that spring

is not just for skinny kids in
ubiquitous highly-strung jeans.

Walking past the gardens
at the end of our village
in the last small field
before the marsh begins
is a still brown horse
in the February sunshine

two boys play in the same
field in the same sun
as though to have each other
and the animal on one side
of the same equation proves
a conspiracy of things.

Walking past the gardens
at the end of our village
crocuses break the path's black mud;
two cats lose their eyes
on nothing, and a tree
from last month's gale
settles forever among the reeds

the noise of summer is beginning,
the boys, the horse and the flowers
are written side by side;
and I go between them, shouting
between them, to hear myself
echo at the end of God's sleeve.

FEBRUARY

This weather lengthens inch by inch
and now the shift of sun and moon
happens in a sky grown
wide enough for both.

It is too soon for green:
ivied oak and frost-stiff grass
are black and white like
lino-cuts, and black and white
like lino-cuts we hang from this
on parachutes of breath.

It is too soon for contact:
profile to profile we live
on necks too cold to turn;
but in this sky, grown wide
enough for both, are learning.

We are the indigenous who feel
beneath our feet the spring beginning,
and in a sky grown wide enough
for summer, dream
small clouds of colour
gathering just below our sight.

They tell me the house stinks,
that calling children crawl
across the floor at the risk
of hands and knees, and that
a pregnant relative ran from
its greased kitchen vomiting.

They tell me she is gin-sodden,
hunched, limping on a foot
which was broken and never set,
and that he is a debris
of used strength and dead hope.

I know that on a wall behind
one locked door a bride waits
in a trailing gown, and that
under lace caps her maids'
eyes surround her. I know
an anthem played them home.

It would be nice to hear
choirboys, or even boozy singing
from the Liberal Club;
it would be nice to hear children
and smell Sunday mornings.

Once, he fed his roses warm
pig's blood, and she washed
caked red from her mouth and nose:
the roses were fat that summer
and in a week her face had healed.
It was an ordinary marriage
which shrieked on Saturdays.

Now they tell me this couple
who pampered my childhood
sit like two piles of discarded
clothing across each other's past,
which closes upon them like the
hoofprints and dung of old animals.

TRANSUBSTANTIATION

I can do without bread
I am overweight in any case
and loathe the way it nails me
to this place without even
a memory of growing corn

that bloody birth symbol –
This is my body! I'm on
the same table waiting for the thing
which will eat me!

What a meal to worship –
eaten and eaten and then eaten
and eaten again, like a live nest
of carved loaves chewing
their way back to the centre.

★

The baker's in Dulwich
where we sat on the warm paving stones
and ate bread pudding

and the other one
where the girl stood on her hands
and showed waving legs –

we were older then.

Long before the days
of Wheaten and Granary
Slimcea and Sandwich Cut

bread was just bread
and you spread it and ate it.

Things will never be that small again.

★

This is our Give-us-this-day bread
which we eat from each other
doubting that there is enough
for everyone and hoping that
eating may maintain love.

My daughter and I have chosen
a fast stream where the fish
are hidden and the birds bombard
their fry with empty bellies.

'There is no bread but bread,' I tell her
'and hunger is its prophet.'

★

In heaven, eating bread will bring us
closer – how could it be otherwise?

In heaven, we will take root eating bread
and grow together for the duration of the meal.

I hope I will eat bread with my daughter
in heaven, for this is what eating bread is about.

It will make up for the bread I have eaten here
which is piled loaf upon loaf around me

like a wall which will feed no-one
not even two little fishes.

Somewhere you have been
sixteen and this is a loss
I live with. I do not
understand the way
the world goes round these
things, as though I have
got this far and must go on.

Thirty years later is not
the same. I cannot even
remember my name thirty
years ago. The world
goes round these things
like a spider's thread: soon
it will suck you out and
leave you hanging dry.

Somewhere you have been
sixteen. Letters, old
photographs and names
keep covering the tracks
between us. I have
stabbed your lovers
with a long knife, but
lacerated only you. Now
jealousy winds you tight
around me – already your
toes and fingertips
are turning blue.

Travelling, you used
the scenery as a barricade,
not knowing we would
touch and make a moon;
ten years too late
that light has reached
me here, and every whitened
bone begins to burn.

But somewhere you have been
sixteen and I do not understand
the way the world goes round
these things – as though
because I have come this far
and must go on, all the time
we've ever known still turns
between us and you have been
sixteen since it began.

ENOUGH IS ENOUGH

It is quiet now:
the river is within its banks again,
leaving a mess of
rubbish above its floodline

the surface is black, glassy,
opaque and could go down
for miles without a hint

we pass each other slowly,
no more than lapping
against clothing, and
we talk like leaves lost
in a side current

our memories have already
chosen one curl of white water,
a moment's rush and a
black branch with a pale wound

we know, as we know names,
the way broken water is
an anger which shows us
down to its oozy bed

but in these times of inactivity
we stop ourselves just where
the air stops, where insects stay
where the stars end their light
and the night pretends.

AWAY

Now, in our separation
that green anorak becomes
a fetish. Bent over
raked soil it hoes weeds
with a peasant patience
turning its hood to understand
the round-robin demands
of a white cat. On clear
days I can see the effect
of its seams, the steel gleam
of zips and the fingertip
touch of nylon promise;
then its padded warmth
pats my shoulder like
a child's comforter.
And, though I no longer
know if this is truth,
the way the winter sun
sometimes flames the face
of the black Tas, I turn
you towards me and each detail
of that gift is bare.

SUNDAY WITH YOU

That river's edge where the reeds
grow out of a marsh-stream
and I could walk there because of the drought

last year's straw crackling
and the debris from the river
lying about drained:
    a carpet of skeletons,
    all the 'dear Elizabeths' said by someone else

that field where we have seen everything,
a spaced line of herons,
a stoat shopping
from one hole to another
and a rabbit screaming from a weasel's lovebite:
    your hand in mine

and this is the lobotomy:
    a small brown bird flying
    inches above the marsh-stream
    weaving to avoid the reeds

it is hot
the drought goes on
forcing a sickness of flowers which drop in a day:
    you move away

and I know I may never leave this place
where everything is dying
so help me God.

LEDA

I don't know why:
I look at the things I can do,
the smoke-mist blowing
across the river and myself
on the other side

such small things under my nose:
a moorhen running across water,
insects which fly on it and stay dry;
whatever happens deep in the reeds
to splash or flutter
on one choked cry

there is a need to stay close here
avoiding that swan who drifts through
with her head above all this,
held as though
the world gives her everything

when I come back to you
I want to know where you were
who you were with
and what you felt about it there;
what are you anyway?

the things I do are nothing;
down here your hair points
to the sea like Ophelia's
and something probes the cracks
between those eyes

but stay here:
I promise I won't drown you with me
if you, in turn, remember
that I will never fly.

OUR LAST WATER-HOLE

It is nothing:
a place where the Tas
bellies into a pond
and goes thin again

it is black water
covering both loss and gain
and showing neither.

I have learned to call the trees alders
which we have changed
with our woven dust sheets

and the smell of semen still
excites the evening's musk.

It is that last meeting place
which we will decorate
for something to begin, realizing
how hard it is for us
to think of not thinking:

there is the memory here
of a buffalo watching
wild dogs rip its life away
which we shared, godlike, through
a telescope and a thousand miles
of pain: this and other evenings –

we are careless about the things we know.

So much has poured into
the holes we are made to carry
that somehow it contains us:

the ground where we drink slopes
into black mud

there is an awareness of others
waiting to be shared

this is where I let you go, not certain
that I can spread so thin

and knowing that the buffalo
was alone among strangers.

WHY WE POPPED TAR

The tar bubbles in the road
burst when you pressed them
leaving your fingers black
which only butter would remove

the sun was black and sticky
as thick as the butter which you
rubbed on your fingers and as
uncomfortable as a wet nappy

mummy was away; if you lay
very still the wet did not matter
but you moved and it was too late
and the black shapes walked off the walls

why you popped the tar was
because it looked like liquorice
and when you stopped the sun made you feel
the street was long and empty

once on that corner a dog lay
in the centre of a crowd of people
and you peered through their legs
and saw a puddle of thick blood

all that day there was dog's blood
at the bottom of your plate
and you ate slowly, not speaking about it;
the dog was mostly black and kept moving

streetcorners were the saddest places
you knew, except for the rooms
where you lived which had old toys
and books chewed at their corners by a dog

that's why you went out in the sun
to break tar bubbles and see the ox-cart
bringing beef suet and once a week
the jamjar roundabout man

and hated rain which stopped up
the windows with tears which
brought the pain up from your belly
and printed it on the wallpaper's brown leaves.

New Poems

AT THE MUSÉE D'ART NAÏF

At the bottom of a hill in Montmartre
where you look up to the church and
the crawling cable cars is a signpost
which directs you to the Musée d'Art Naïf.

Above it there is always a small halo
of blue sky or if it rains the rain falls
in straight rods of silver and the winds
blow around it in perfect circles of
whistling breath and nearby someone sings
through a window which is not quite closed.

There, if you walk in the direction the sign-
post shows, past small shops that look as though
they are used, saying Bonjour to the people
who use them, you are glad to be in Montmartre
in clean air looking for the Musée d'Art Naïf.

And you will find, where the rain stops and
there is a smell of sunshine, a small building
which is not labelled but has two galleries
of paintings and a well-behaved sheep which
baas quietly from a pen in the wet-scrubbed
foyer beside a turnstile, a tiny café and
a ticket lady with an early-morning face.

In the gallery d'Art Naïf the pictures are
arranged in countries and you can walk through
Europe spending an hour in Czechoslovakia.
And every portrait looks like someone
and there are families working in fields
or in farms among animals with familiar faces
and angels come and go in the Garden of Eden
where the sun shines in the middle of the sky
and you can see each leaf plainly on every tree.

And on certain weekdays a crocodile of children
invade the Musée d'Art Naïf to call the dozing
sheep awake and run among the portraits
and the animals and the angels coming and going
in the sunshine in the Garden of Eden.

And when they leave, the silence in the Musée
d'Art Naïf in the middle of Montmartre on an
ordinary morning is like the silence of the
world on the seventh day of Creation when
everything is astonished at what it has become.

POOR OLD EDWARD GOT BOGGED DOWN

(In memory of Edward Barker, sculptor)

First of all in days
the way they came upon him
not always comfortably
but with little edges
hidden behind the familiar

where desperately or merely depressed
he hid inside the dovecote
dodging the cooings and droppings
or walked with the whole tribe
of lost cats to the pond
and the overreaching gunnera tree
where his small feet sank
into the marshy grass

or named the weeds which
grew head-high beside the house
hiding the spiky goddesses
he made to poke between them
into the wide East Anglian sky

but poor old Edward
got bogged down in
the moments which he laid
between the minutes
of every day and became
not alone but lonely in them
and finally afraid

and tried to turn his goddesses
into a crowd of warm round ladies
with a little tickle
and a lot of comfort
and took to watching them

at bus stops or beside
the railway platforms where
they left work each day
to make predictable journeys home

and in the moments between the
minutes rattled the grate
in a cloud of ashes
and waited for depression
to settle into fear

and hid in the weeds
until walking time
and watched and worried
and sadly died of one
last spiteful thrust
from one of his mean
old spiky women
who had grown into
a weed beside the house
waiting for this
last sharp moment to come.

ON SAYING NO

Today, in the ninth year of
Margaret Thatcher's Britain,
a pale young man, cold, looking as though
he were withdrawing from something serious
said, quietly: Excuse me.

The weather man had not predicted snow
but the wind had a worrying look.
Kingsway seemed ruler-straight between
unemployment and a failing National Health Service.
The Russians were showing a fur-clad lady to
our figurehead. The newspapers were unfriendly.

The young man, looking seriously withdrawn,
said Excuse me. He was wearing a white
plastic hat, summery, out of season, and
he shivered as though something was shaking him
inside. He said Excuse me, quietly,
Could you give me something to get some food?

Cheated, I took my eyes away from him.
Saying No as quietly as he'd asked, I walked away,
not knowing why I'd said No except it seemed
the reasonable thing to do, knowing nobody
starves in Britain today, that he had not seemed
badly dressed or old or anything like that.

I spoke to myself. I said: I have worked
for forty of my sixty years, one third
of all I've earned has gone in tax,
I've bought flags when I could not avoid
the seller's eyes. I am normally generous.

I do not know why I said No. Perhaps
from embarrassment. But I wished the young man
would walk past me again and say Excuse me again.
I wished for that piece of history to be replayed.

Looking back along Kingsway, he had gone.
I think the weather man may have been wrong.
I do not know why the newspapers are so unfriendly.
Nor why our streets are so badly maintained.

1939

It always seemed as if
a film were beginning: dark road,
the motorbike-and-sidecar
weaving on it, then the titles.

Back home the Boys' Brigade were blowing
silver bugles at Church Parade
and the Lifeboys walked
behind them like soldiers.

For the rest of the year
nobody hit me. As though when
somebody died, there was
an amnesty on chastisement.

★

That summer there was ice-cream and
sunshine on the Isle of Wight.
Out on the story-blue sea
warships whizzed and whooped.

My fair skin itched in the sun.
In the holiday camp we sat
with the same two ladies every day
and sang the camp songs:

Goodnight campers don't sleep in your braces.
Goodnight campers put your teeth in Jeyes's.
No more sorrow, bring the empties back tomorrow.
Goodnight campers, Goodnight.

★

At Christmas they bought me
an expensive Hornby speedboat.

On Horniman's Pond
it sailed alone on black water.

*

For a few months the dancesongs
made my mother weep:
Tonight, tonight I must forget,
Music Maestro please.

And when the war began
our class sang: Fleas, fleas
with great big hairy knees,
as we crocodiled from home.

*

At the end of the year
Rockfist Rogan RAF
replaced The Boxing Bargee.

My mother suddenly stopped
weeping, and the amnesty
on chastisement ended.

There were no proper war songs
but they sang the camp songs quietly
on the Isle of Wight.

My fair skin itched in bright sunlight.
Racer III sailed Horniman's Pond
alone on black water.

And on a dark road between Winchester
and Southampton a motorbike-and-sidecar
waited for the titles to begin.

Grown-ups used to stop and watch us fly
those aeroplanes: cardboard wing and
fuselage and a small lead nose-weight,
we catapulted them with an elastic band
threaded through a metal peg. Grown-ups
stopped and watched them soar roof-high
and loop the loop and swoop into
a flattened dive which landed them
at our feet again and again and again.

They cost a ha'penny with half a dozen
sweet cigarettes and we only bought them
when their fashion came around and
it was glider time. At other times we
made aeroplanes from folded paper which
sometimes flew, or else we abandoned
aeroplanes altogether and went back to
fivestones, foursticks, tinny or tipcat.

But when we flew those cardboard aeroplanes
grown-ups stopped to watch us and explain the
models they had made from printed plans and
balsa wood and dope and a long rubber motor
with a mechanical winder which they entered
for competitions in a monthly magazine
called *Aeromodeller* or something like that.

But we were never really interested; we
never knew why those sweetfag aeroplanes
flew the way they did, and we grew out of them.
Just as there came a time when we could
no longer close our eyes tight against
bright sunlight and live in its blood-red world
where insects buzzed head-high and we saw
God look at us and laugh and say Goodbye.

THE SEA, THE SEA

In a house
at the edge of a cliff
you can hear the sea
even with the windows closed

but at night
in your small bedroom
with the green and brown leaves
rustling the wallpaper
you leave the window open
to the wind
and even in your sleep
hear the sea slap and suck
and the pebbles running back
to where they were made

but the edge of the world
is crumbling
and houses with both closed and open windows
fall into the sea
with shops and churches
which according to legend
still sound their bells in storms

and in those smug houses
which are safe from erosion
the sea
even with its windows open
and the wind at its back
whispers so far away
it is lost in the conversation of dreams

until now
with so little time left
almost any empty house will do
near or far from the sea
even if you have to change the wallpaper.

THAT WAR

At a time
when there were simply adults
and they were one age

at a time
when the War of the Worlds
was about to begin

at a time
of the wireless
and the rained-on cinema
when all Governments
wore uniforms or top hats

at a time
when the last long summer
had not even weakened into autumn

we were sent away
with two sandwiches
and a farting gas-mask
in a cardboard box

at a time
when home was where our schoolfriends were
we did not even think
of crying

but slept on straw
and planned Midnight Feasts
with two biscuits
and an Individual Fruit Pie

our second stop
was the seaside
where one November day
on the first empty beach I knew

silver-scaled sprats flew
like Spitfires
the sun glinting on
their diving wings

this was our only war
our ration you might say
and it is important
to have this memory

of Billy Bishop attacking
out of the sun
with his synchronised gun
blazing through a blurred propeller
and the stench of fish.

There was a job which went
Monday Tuesday Wednesday
Thursday Friday, as though
gold watches were hallmarked
St. Peter with an eternal
guarantee; there was a bed
which went babies, toddlers,
schoolboys, teenagers and
Goodbye; a woman whose waiting
went lover, wife, sister,
mother, furniture and saint;
alcohol, hangovers, trains,
tubes, buses and weeks of rain;
but there was nothing which
ever said This is all there is.

'So the person I'm looking at now
is not really you', the well-dressed
pretty psychiatrist said.

'Oh no!
No, no, no!
I've been ill,'
the sad mouse said
from the folds of
her meaningless clothes.

'When I'm not ill
I'm Princess Diana,
chased by Prince Charles
to Westminster Abbey.
The Queen is my mother,
and the hippies in Wales
have made *me* their Queen.

'Oh no! No, this
is not me,' she said
looking wistfully down
like the rest of us.

Then there were voices
from the walls of our room:
'It is normal to hear voices,'
the voices said. And
unseen music fiddled
the face of Diana.

'I'm me! I'm me! I'm me!'
the pretty psychiatrist sang,
as she took her fee
and went back to her husband
who was an adman
and probably drank.

THE BALL WAS OVER

For at least a year
there was a priest, a solicitor,
a doctor, an accountant,
an editor and a man
who mended windows.
It was the year of
getting our lives together.

For at least a year
this long retinue
of retainers was
the family I supported.
Each of them frightened me:
like a child I gave up sweets
to keep my teeth white,
like an oriental I worked
hard for my elders;
I ate an apple on the day
I did not see my doctor and
prayed when the priest was away.

That was the year of
getting our lives together,
beyond the pleasure principle,
where you need
all the guides you can get.
I explained my accountant to my
bank manager, my doctor to my
priest, my wife to my
solicitor and could not pay
the man who mended windows.

After words failed me
the editor left and the accountant
stopped counting my cheques,
my wife checked out with

the solicitor and my doctor said:
Why worry, it's all in the mind.
I did not want to lose the priest
but once the church had crumbled
there was nowhere for God to go.

That was the year we got
our lives beyond pleasure, using
all the memories we could get.
After the long hot summer
the days were shorter,
the horizons were tired and
late in December our dreams
kissed us Goodbye.
One of them was recurring
and in a voice like my own
said over and over:
Shorter days mean longer nights
and I know that pleasure
is cheaper than principle
but it does not last,
it does not last.

NUNC DIMITTIS

In his sleep the cows
drift through the old streets
filling the frost
with their breathing.

A voice is explaining itself
to someone who does not
need an explanation or
who has died without it.

He has justified every failure
by believing that
anything here can be
used to make a shelter.

He has chosen eight discs.
The seabirds cry through
the old streets. 'Would
you be able to look after

yourself, catch fish or
build a boat?' Someone is
thanking him over and over
again. Over and over.

It is turning-out time
in the big bar of the Savoy Tavern.
Safe inside our last-ordered pints
we glaze the tartan walls and
the carpet's red-squared anonymity.

No more than the murmur of a swell
whose tide is turning backgrounds
the chink of gathered glasses and
the slosh of legal ablutions.

Toilets flush, smoke is sucked through
breezy open doors. Groups break up
and drift with the tide, leaving
isolated solitary drinkers draining
their last minutes away.

                    One of these
whose shortness circles his beer-drinking
pregnancy rolls a fag from a pewter-
coloured tin and, as though he is in labour,
sucks in and whistles out the little air
the brewers and tobacco barons have
left him. Then, the effort over, fag
rolled and beer bolted, is a kind of
calm, settled in an island of his
dying self.

             Half of me, in my
smart-arsed class-jumping awareness,
condemns, 'You fool.... you bloody fool!'
The other half, sad and sailing, whispers,
'Jesus Christ.... how I envy you!'

NOTHING DIES

The doctors finally caught up
with my poor old Woodbine aunt:
dragged her from her barstool
in the Palace pub (Don't sit
there, it's Nancy's) and took her
to a table in St Mary's.

For a month she argued back:
'It's only a toe,' she said
watching her foot turn black.
'Live or die,' they answered
'Live or die.' She wasn't sure
which choice to make: her ginny
living had always seemed so close
to giving up the ghost. 'Try
this for size,' they said, measuring
her blackened leg for a plastic
fantasy. 'Sign here please,'
they ordered and she signed.

Later in a wheelchair in a
flat for the disabled
she complained of a pain in her
absent pickled toe.
'What you talking about, you
ain't got no bleedin toe,' her
sister's voice explained, hoping
exegesis would contain the mystery.

Phantom pain, O phantom pain!
no surgeon's saw is sharp enough
to cut that out. Her leg still
talks to its plastic part.
The body's dumb!
I once saw in a photograph
a tree insisting that its broken

leaf was whole, filling the space
with a hazy memory,
confirming that the resurrection
still promises our bodies back,
as though the soul creates some
shape to make its presence felt.

Worldwide are the ways we overcome
our flesh, with yoga or with motor
cars. The Sun also rises on a
photograph of tit and bum. We succumb
to the faith of transubstantiation.

So barely living when she was alive
my poor old gin and Woodbine aunt
has one foot in her grave, whose
pain will penetrate the puzzle:
waiting there with God knows what
new shoe to carry her in glory
through the great gates of her time.

To make bread you take
flour, water, yeast, some
salt and bake it. To catch
fish you hang a line where
fish are and drag them out.
Historically it is better
if the loaves are made from
barley and the fish dried
but probably any fish and bread
will do and there are
excellent ones in Sainsbury's.
The difficulty begins when
even with 3 million unemployed
you cannot find 5000 hungry
people to watch you break
the bread and divide the fish.
This miracle became redundant
2000 years ago, and was
never popular. A few people
still meet to talk and sing
about it and you can't blame
them for that nor for the way
they drive home afterwards.
Nobody's sorrier than they
are about the way the bread,
the fish and the people will not
get up and walk around but
they know that even if they did
somebody would gather them up
and sell them back for
a week's work and that
somehow there will always be
about 3 million unemployed.

THE HEROES

'After the war....say, "I fought and marched
with the Desert Army"'   (Winston Churchill)

Who is this old man
in a Basque onion-seller's hat
blowing cracked notes on a bugle?

Why is he standing in desert sand
with a lopsided look on his shopkeeper's face
and trinkets on his jacket?

He is a comedian.

No. Wait. The camera is pulling away.
He is not alone. Other old men
are around him, uncomfortably formal,
looking where the lens is pointing.

It is a troupe of clowns.

They are marching, no they are walking
in file between small concrete mounds.
Somebody is holding a flag.

Wait. Listen. A voice is talking from a cloud.
They are the old men of history:
pennants pinned on a bedroom wall,
free from the Daily Mail.
They are Our Side.

The old comedian is talking in a funny voice
to a clean face lined with elocution.
It all comes back: Hearts of Oak,
true grit, jolly good, gather round
the donkeys.

Where are the actors now who played
Rommel and Monty? Where, for Chrissake,
is the Director?

Unrehearsed, the fools cannot find
the right names on the right graves,
are raising their glasses vaguely
above any old concrete mound.

And the camera has pulled back too far,
is framing them in dry space. See:
this is no cast of thousands,
it is a shuffle of survivors
the programme pulled together for a few pounds.

Here is a token Kraut in a costume cap:
'Vee should neffer enemies haff been!'
Here is a close-up of a tight-lipped
handshake.

Now poppies are falling from
the Albert Hall and Eddie Calvert
is playing a golden trumpet,
lest we forget an institution.

Hard of hearing,
the old men no longer know
what their loud leaders are shouting about.

They do not understand
that war is dead, and tomorrow
will bring only a collision of deterrents.

They hang tunelessly
on the last note of their old bugle,
certain that some memory
of something will survive.

OCTOBER ANECDOTE

(For Neil)

In Norwich Castle's clean museum
they have glassed in all the birds
that ever flew. I don't know them all –
a few torn tits the cats bring in,
red on shades of green and blue, and
one owl I recognise from headlights
on the winding drive back home.

Tennyson's eagle clasps a crag
in a corner of the wall, facing the ducks
which call at night from our millpond.
Others I've known only from photographs.

Repatriated here alongside Cotman,
Seago, Crome, a short-haired man in a
council suit guards them from girls
in shocking woollen socks.

I'm sure they never flew. I can't
believe they kestrelled the wind, nor
tore their talons through that posed
duckling. As dust dulls the tips of their
feathers and films their eyes, they are
learning the words on their captions.

Outside, shoppers fall from castle walls;
from the cathedral the angels rise.
There is no wind here, but the air dries
such a mummified affinity, I cannot stare
too long at them, nor they at me.

GARDENING NOTES

We are trying to put the spring back
into the garden, which dark nights and
hard frosts have loosened like teeth.

It should not matter. The moorhen
would still walk here without flowers, and
the walls of the house will not fall down.

It is more for our own hands to do something
with the landscape – exiles that we are:
only here because the plants ignore us.

We are the great running away which would not
wait for the city to stop. It is our history
we are making for the moles to push aside.

Forgive us our straw hats and private humour.
Forgive the way we stand together for our
photograph. It is our only camouflage.

We are trying to put the spring back, aware
of the way the land rolls by without us, and
that what we grasp is only our time as it goes.

GENESIS

My mother must have
pointed her out to me,
navy-blue serge
on an old black bike
on some grey winter day
when even the dogs were indoors,
saying: Look, there's Nurse
Winnie who delivered you!

There was rime frost on
the tarred road her black legs
flew over; her eyes streamed,
her nose glowed and she blew
white breath like a train
travelling between pains.

Of course I didn't see it
that way then: there was
just an old girl on an
old bike who waved.
The rest is written in by me
to make the event important.

And yet the nappy scar
which now sprouts a single hair
is true. It *was* cold,
and I do remember wondering
whether she was hurrying to
that great nursery where
all the gooseberry bushes grew.

AT HOME

This is a used country kept flat
by God so that the cows can eat it

A place to sleep where at night
mushrooms leap from its dreaming edges

Where to exclude myself I make and
keep it as a place to go from

Its damp evenings bring a confusion
of bats to our late house martins

Norfolk breathes and the summer's weed
weaves a green runner going nowhere

From the house the fifties jazz I choose
returns its running notes to where I am

Looking for landmarks along this line
trying to discover where it was and when.

'Can I have your old brown coat?'
my daughter asks. One that I bought
fifteen, twenty years ago
in a Marks & Spencer sale.
Nothing fashionable, not even
in the strange way she makes
old fashions come around again.
This is a cotton zip-up thing
that was never out of fashion
because never in. Washed and
pressed by me, you can see,
with the collar up, the change
of tone the sun's bleached in.
It has worn well and worn into
me, so that I wear it without
thinking for gardening or midweek
morning shopping sprees and, like
skin, it doesn't wear out visibly.
Puzzled and reluctant to let it go,
I ask her why she wants it.
'It's an heirloom,' she tells me,
and suddenly I know the irony
of being nineteen, when everything
about everything is new and all sin
is original. When life seems to
begin wherever it happens to be
on some particular Saturday
without that sense of inevitability
we call religion or commitment.
Commitment to what? Religious
about what? What a fuckup
we must have made of things
when a brown St Michael
jacket becomes an artefact.
Some sort of shadow on the sun
has made the day seem older.

Three-score-years-and-ten....
it leaves me fifteen more to go.
Presumably it won't wear out by then.
I'll will it to her if she needs it so.

WHY WE LOOK FOR MUSHROOMS

Walking across the recreation ground
on the South Coast of England
in wartime with the sound of shingle
not quite in my ears and all the
coloured pennants locked away
for the grey years which would
take me from boyhood to the Navy
with no living in between,
I saw my first bright white mushroom
unmagically by a cinder track
and carried it back to my billet
with the gardener's family where
it was fried with their own tomatoes.

The war went on with boredom and
very little fear, most of the fighting
being on the radio and about
other people somewhere else,
and there was very little living
in between the headlines and
the simple maps with arrows.

And afterwards, of course, in the
cold weather which seemed perpetual
between the bombsites which were never
cleared I was pointed at the girl
next door and found two rooms among
the ruins beside an office and a
paper job and made two children
without much living in between.

And imagined in the long love-rationed
nights a soft knock on the rented door
where something I had missed might
lead me by another hand to such
bright white mushrooms as have never
been before and the sound of the shingle
by green pennants flying and the smell
of mushrooms frying with our own tomatoes.

CAMPANOLOGY

Bells are nothing to enjoy:
they break you from a dawdle
to a sweat from seven streets away

or in prattling choirs tell the street
your play will be
Sunday-neat and sad.

They lay like iron bars across
the public park ringing
favourite hymns but never singing

or in their peals rush each other
like iron men bringing bedlam
to unsuspecting souls.

Darlings of respectability they
drag the tired from their beds
and callously deafen hunchbacks,

or handheld are the loneliness
of lepers telling nightmares
through shutters or barred doors.

Bells are nothing to enjoy:
it took a war to silence them
and even then they threatened –

we knew they were Hitler's column
longing to rattle robot tongues
and bring him home.

COMMUNION

Each season brings its own loneliness:
this morning the three bells ring
through frost. It is the temperature,
I tell myself, which keeps us
so deep and slowly moving, and
know that I am lying.

On the other side of the mist
an animal sounds muffled and far away.
The filtered sun shows its own slow beauty
and, just out of sight, the day shines.
Dearly beloved, the grass is always
greener where the others pray.

At night the stubble burns in long lines
of orange flame, making black pathways
to winter's shortest day where,
at the maze heart, we find a cup,
some old bread and a little wine.

Nobody said we must feel this love,
only that it is beyond our understanding.
Nobody said we must be happy,
only that at the end of this mystery
something is about to happen which depends
upon our lives and our forgiveness.

MATINS

The tide is out at Manningtree
and queues of white seabirds
wait for something to surface
from the black mud.
Beyond the estuary the fields
roll slightly as though relieved
to leave flat Norfolk behind.
There is a white mill, a stream
and a sudden yellow crop.

I write these colours in, which
mean nothing to me, whose eyes
opened on the grey slates of wet-
roofed houses in South London.

Our days walked between them
with always an appointment to keep:
quick short steps which stopped dead
on Sundays. In my bed at night
I waited for tomorrow to begin
and sometimes woke crying
because it had not come to meet me.

I remember a horse which fell down
between its shafts and could not
be moved. I remember a black dog
dying on the same street-corner.
And an aeroplane. These have never
been enough, though with them I
have tried to keep a history alive.

Yet Manningtree, whether its estuary
is filled with water or trapped mud,
means nothing to me. This journey
knows where we are going as well
as I do: all I want is for
my voice to leave us alone.

HIS EYES

(In memory of Michael Marais)

He died in a rush
in a car outside his door
leaving the living room empty
and the dogs whining.

He left a woman whose
eyes streamed through
the first hard winter
and on into that damp spring.

He left restless pets,
the sad mad he ministered to,
and the powerful binoculars
he drove the length
of England to buy.

In October his wife
gave them to me with books
on birds and a subscription
to the RSPB.

I am no birdman;
abandoned on a bedroom table
they reproach me
with their blindness.

Outside my window the birds
fly; I recognise the small
house martins which arrive
in May, ragged crows,
pheasants thick until July,
peewits and the gaudy tits.

Probably if pressed I could
name more – those which
I see myopically
against the garden green
or circular Norfolk sky.

I know his ground-glass
miracles could bring them
near enough to touch and,
feather by feather, I'd
categorise them from
his books.

I do not try.
I do not want to make them
such a large part of my view,
perhaps prefer my blurred
weak-eyed impression.

In any case, like the dogs,
he was their lord and master
and I, alive in dead men's shoes,
do not wish to lift
the pennies from his eyes.

White on dark water, so stark
I leave my binoculars behind
and watch with bare red eyes

two swans, taut in sexuality,
stretching their necks
alternately side by side.

They are early: colour is
still to come to bone-dry rushes
and trees bank black strangling

their green. It is a hard wedding:
sharp brambles and ivy-covered
stumps hunch and hug;

sleet pokes the surface from
a blank neutrality, to come back
spitting with all its mouths.

Roused, the spread wings
beat their own storm towards
the north, wing against wind.

Somewhere in all this a small
heat is held, like the hope
of a cold man drowning.

The weather is with us, like a
long March of sharp winds and
a late frost. Grey light on flat
fields with scarcely the headroom
to clear an upright corpse.
God knows our mood and chastises us.
We are moving into the day of
families: voices are everywhere, as
interchangeable as new clothes.
'Who saw him die? What did he say?'
groping for the one lie
to build on stone. These are our
circles. A wood I walked through once:
rooks, rabbits and a hedgehog
swinging from a head-high branch
whose stench I knew before I saw them.
Spent cartridges on trodden ground
and around us a deafman's silence of
internal sounds. We are moving into
the day of funerals of old men whose
lives will neither burn nor rot into
useful loam. My black tie is worn
for the wake that will follow, in a
front room, behind curtains, up a road.

On the way I heard Whistling Rufus
performed by a station porter
on a miles-from-anywhere platform
on the Norfolk-Suffolk border.

The wind and water of East Anglia
caged us in late winter; doors
slammed on it and we waited for
our time to come. Whistling Rufus

was six feet tall, raw-boned and
walked in a way that described porters:
he held his watch in one hand,
whistle in the other and as we

rolled away blew this chorus
between them. For half the length
of the platform his tune tied us to
bent grass and birds tumbling on

the teeming wind – until each note
broke away and we too were
blown up the same coastline.
I hadn't heard that tune whistled

since I was a boy: it was like
some great John Henry calling across
the flat sky to where trains turn
on timetables and old ladies doze.

ANY QUESTIONS

The old poet is on a platform in
a hall in the centre of the city;
two other poets are on his left hand
and a neat chairman on his right.

Each poet has read, in rotation, twice;
each has signed books and made
nicely-phrased noises at nicely-made
faces. Now they have finished.

Applause dies a natural death, and
the chairman, feeling that each performance
should have its coda, a theme to tap toes to
on various journeys, asks for questions.

A silence grows uncomfortably long which
the chairman breaks with a practised
provocation, filling the hall with
a kind of loud cocktail chatter.

The old poet takes no part in this: he looks
at his feet and discovers loose wool at the top
of one of his socks; he frowns and pulls at it
until a young eager voice addresses him by name.

He, the speaker, would eagerly like to know...
etcetera and etcetera. The wool at the top
of the sock still resists the poet's fingers;
he gives it up and sits quietly. The audience sits

quietly, waiting. The death the old man has faced
in every poem gathers around him; the landscape
he made in five days threatens the room,
and he struggles out of it with a terrible inertia

to overcome. He faces the darkness piled upon him
and remains dumb. The audience fidgets and begins to go,
the chairman blows kisses at their backs, and the show
gathers itself to go on the road again.

OUR WAR

We stopped on Hong Kong's
winding coastal road and the
Chinese driver showed us foxholes.

I remember the scraps of uniform but not
whether the bones and dogmeat flesh
were fact or fiction.

It is Christmas in Hong Kong
in 1946, at the end of
the war we just missed.

I do not remember celebration,
unless the NAAFI sold mince pies
and we gave each other cards,

or plunged ourselves into
the sacking-draped beds
where pox was sold, and

the old married men carried
it back to the sickbay
in paper, singing carols.

Hardly mountaineering:
Saturday families jump across it,
three generations and a dog; the café owner
makes its point in a faded Ford;
we sip his tea, eat beans on toast,
people of the plains. And yet
the Midland winds lean on Wales
and we have fourteen counties in our pocket
to spend on change. It is not enough:
we know the shrunken world's a visual trick
which grows towards us
and that around any bend
we could meet two people walking,
the size of despair.

REEDHAM MARSHES

(For Eric, John and the Lizzies)

They say the water's salt here
as though the North Sea's fingers
are at our belly, tickling us like trout.

Dozy from blue and bottle-green,
we wallow in each passing wash
like a long drunk on a hot Saturday.

The reeds sigh and part as we enter them,
then zip us up behind like some
silk Sargasso. It is an old fantasy.

Sick from a seized engine, we sit
in this sanctuary of seabirds where
at night the crocodiles slip from holes

in their reed bed to jostle us
like hissing logs; and we confuse
the red rising moon with its setting sun.

Now no longer water-borne we drift
on this night mist which dreams us:
there are sharp cries, quiet splashes

and the voices of fishermen in an old pub
where a hand pours a White Shield Worthington
as clear as a bell and without a hint of mud.

THE NATURE OF MEMORY

On a day which
might as well be Monday
in a small house in a poor street
a dog which
might as well be our mongrel
went mad in the kitchen.
Drooling white froth mixed with blood
from the lip it had torn on a nail
it yelped in circles and jumped
as high as a man up the kitchen wall.
I was five and
I was not afraid until
the woman who might as well be my mother
screamed It's mad! It's mad! and ran
from the room slamming the door
loudly and finally behind her.

This is memory: it is winter and
the afternoon light is fading outside.
I am in a room and
a dog is trying to jump the wall.
It is stupid after half a century
to pretend I can remember
anything of fear. But perhaps just as
stupid to pretend there was nothing.
Today there are simply facts to recall:
   1. the dog had drunk disinfectant
      and was burning inside
   2. my father came home and drowned him
      in the stone copper
   3. my mother joked about
      shutting the dog and me together
   4. I was five. That is all.

Fifty years is almost a period of history;
the man who drowned the dog is dead
but his wife is still alive.
There have been children, grandchildren
and one great-grandchild.
Letters have come through the post.
There have been floods, droughts
and even a war. It is stupid to pretend
I can remember anything of fear,
equally stupid to say there was nothing.
Let us call the day Monday,
let us note that it happened,
let us regret the feeling that has
drained from everything, but remember
that it was the dog who died.